Copyright © 2024 Mary Kay Morrison

All Rights reserved. No part of this book may be reproduced or transmitted in any form by any means, electronic or mechanical, including photocopying, recording, or by any information storage and retrieval system, without written permission from the Publisher.

Published by Humor Quest
322 Canary Drive, Caledonia, IL  61011

ISBN: 978-1-7367913-1-8

### Credits:

Editor and Production Designer:
Deborah McKew, *Words in Play*

Cover Artist and Graphics: Kyle Edgell

Photographer: Don Morrison

Portrait of the Author (page x): Jared Silver

# Legacy of Laughter

# The Playbook

## HOW TO NURTURE A HUMOR BEING

*Mary Kay Morrison*

**Photography by Don Morrison**

*Charley,*
*This book would not have been possible without Jill! Grateful for you ♥ and your friendship*
*Love,*
*Mary Kay*

# Contributors

Don Morrison
William Heinisch
Jennifer Heinisch
Andy Heinisch
Julie Heinisch
Rachael Van Heuklon
Jason Van Heuklon
Peter Heinisch
Valerie Heinisch
Richard Wiltz
Jan Jakeway
Deb Gauldin
George Letcher
Barb Best - Joanne Jackal
Ros Ben-Moshe

*Grandchildren*

(*in age order in right photo*)
Faith
Isaiah
Cloe
Steve
Katie
Christine
Maria (Mimi)
Emma
Samuel
Andrew
Tyler
Ben

**AUTHOR'S NOTE:** This book is written with the recognition that the ideas presented here barely scratch the surface of the range of possibilities. There is an appreciation that each parent, grandparent, and other caregivers will use their own special sauce in creating their *Legacy of Laughter*.

This book is dedicated to my incredible husband Don,
>    To my children and their spouses,
>       To my amazing grandchildren who are the motivation for this book,
>          And to all of those who are making a difference in the lives of kids.

# What the Experts Are Saying about The Playbook

*Legacy of Laughter: The Playbook* is brimming with practical insights on laughter and play from the cradle onwards. This handy compact book is designed as a guide, for all ages and levels, on how to harness the power of laughter and play in your life. Its accessible and informative style is no coincidence—this is educator and founding director of the Association of Applied and Therapeutic Humor, Mary Kay Morrison's fourth book. It is not to be missed!

—Dr. Freda Gonot-Schoupinsky, Author
*The Positive Psychology of Laughter and Humour,* University of Bolton United Kingdom

*"... not to be missed!"*

*"... will launch you on a joyful adventure ..."*

Mary Kay's ideas for laughter and play will launch you on a joyful adventure with your children that will last a lifetime. Her insights and anecdotes are spot on and will have you tearing up and laughing at the same time. Humor is the very best medicine!

—Anne Pratt, Director
Red Skelton Museum of American Comedy

*"...this book unleashes the power of humor to uplift lives..."*

Mary Kay's book unleashes the power of humor to uplift lives on both a personal and global scale. This book will replenish your sense of play, rejuvenate your spirit, and inspire you to share play's gifts with the children in your life.

With delightful wit and wisdom, Mary Kay Morrison makes an irresistible case that laughter-filled play is essential for nurturing happy, thriving kids while keeping the inner child in all of us alive.

—*Karyn Buxman, Neurohumorist*
TEDx: *How Humor Can Change the World*

> ... provides creative tools for children of all ages ...

There is no one in the entire world who is more knowledgeable about ways to provide creative tools for reaching children of all ages than Mary Kay Morrison. Founder of the Humor Academy at the Association for Applied and Therapeutic Humor, she crafted a course of study enhancing the understanding of humor development, appropriate uses of humor, and an overview of research in the field.

Her previous Legacy book has added much joy to relationships between grandparents and their grandchildren. This new edition will add guidance for parents, babysitters, and educators for all levels, with the intention of adding improved attention, better retention, and additional joy to any environment.

—Joyce M. Saltman, Ed.D., Professor Emeritus
Special Education, Southern Connecticut State University
Life Member, Certified Humor Professional
Recipient of AATH Lifetime Achievement Award

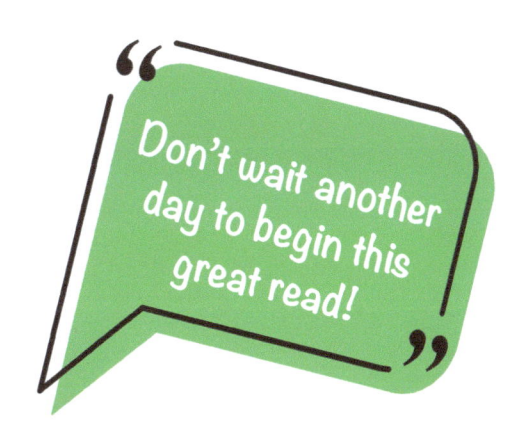

> Don't wait another day to begin this great read!

*Legacy of Laughter; The Playbook* has never-ending suggestions for play activities and looking for the funny in life. Mary Kay is encouraging when she says you are not too old, and it is never too late. Don't wait another day to begin this great read about play that will inspire you to enjoy the challenges of new interests.

—Brenda Elsagher, Author and National Speaker
Certified Humor Professional
Association for Applied and Therapeutic Humor

So, you want more laughter and play in your life—who doesn't? Mary Kay Morrison's latest book, *Legacy of Laughter: The Playbook* offers tips for babies to super-seniors. Go ahead, giggle, wiggle and play away.

—Pat Rumbaugh, Founder
Let's Play America

> Go ahead, giggle, wiggle, and play away.

viii

# Contents

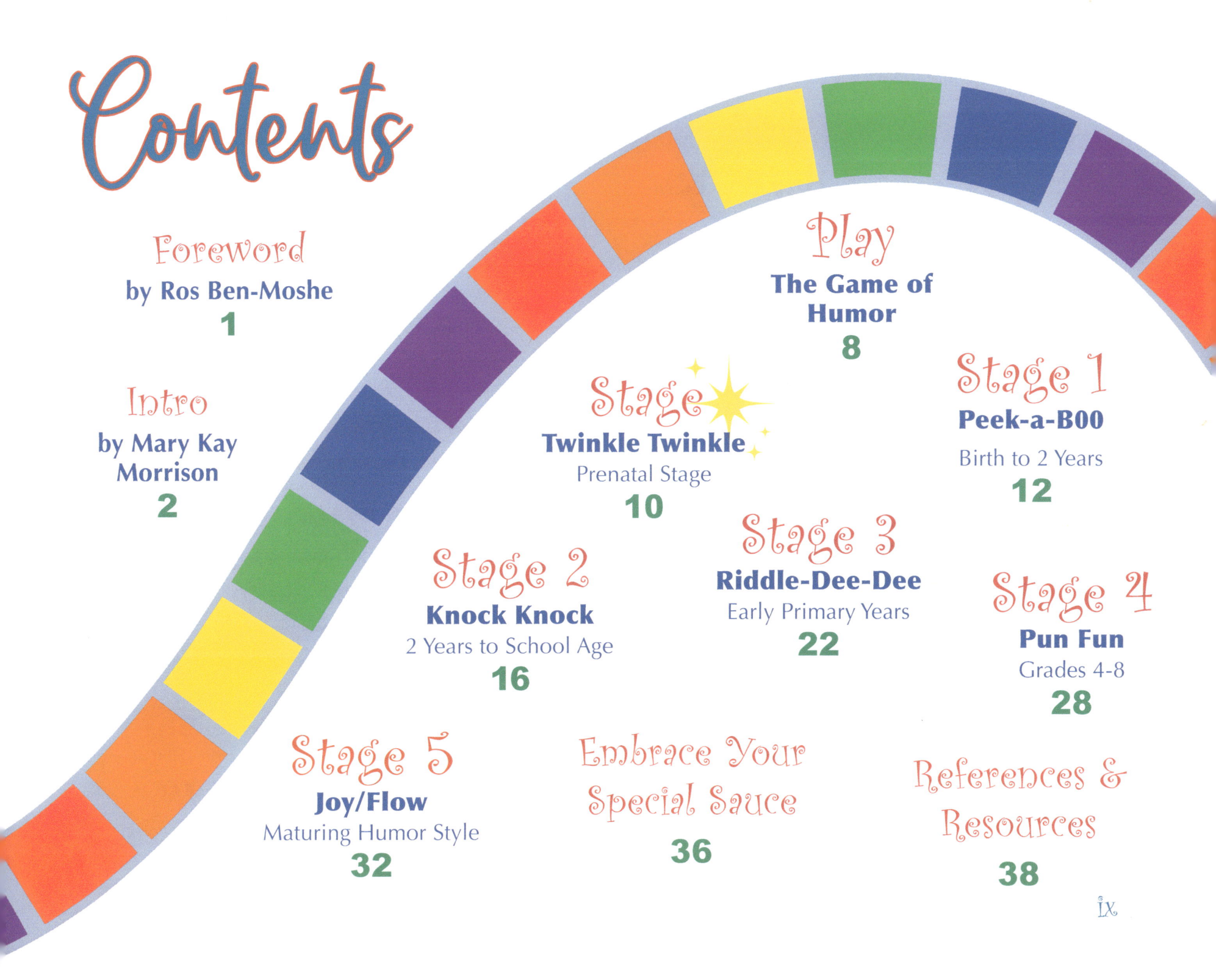

**Foreword**
by Ros Ben-Moshe
1

**Intro**
by Mary Kay Morrison
2

**Play**
The Game of Humor
8

**Stage**
Twinkle Twinkle
Prenatal Stage
10

**Stage 1**
Peek-a-B00
Birth to 2 Years
12

**Stage 2**
Knock Knock
2 Years to School Age
16

**Stage 3**
Riddle-Dee-Dee
Early Primary Years
22

**Stage 4**
Pun Fun
Grades 4-8
28

**Stage 5**
Joy/Flow
Maturing Humor Style
32

**Embrace Your Special Sauce**
36

**References & Resources**
38

ix

## The Impact of Play on Brain Development

| CAGED | CAGED | CAGED | CAGED | |
|---|---|---|---|---|
| No Stimulation | Toys | Friends | Toys and Friends | In the Wild |
| Neural Connections Increase → | | | | |

## The Power of Play

STRESS ↓   PLAY & FUN ↑

## Benefits of Humor, Laughter, and Play

- Reduces stress → Decreases cortisol levels
- Stimulate organs → Enhances oxygen intake
- Improves immune system → Increases endorphins
- Improves mood → Reduces depression/anxiety

*Source: MayoClinic.org*

## The Research is Clear— Play is Good for You!

# Foreword

## by Ros Ben-Moshe

The moment I first met Mary Kay, I was struck by her boundless enthusiasm for life and wholehearted living. She radiated positivity, a quality she generously shared with everyone she encountered. Since then, not only has our friendship blossomed, but she has been a beacon of inspiration in my own professional development.

I have cherished opportunities to collaborate with this passionate educator, author, and co-founder of the Humor Academy at the Association for Applied and Therapeutic Humor. This includes the research project, together with Dr Freda Gonot-Schoupinsky, *Humor, Laughter and Mental Health: A case study of Mary Kay Morrison*, which showcases Mary Kay's evolution in becoming a "humor-being" and her dedication to the advancement of the field of humor research.

*The author (left) with Ros Ben-Moshe*

Mary Kay's first book, *Using Humor to Maximize Learning: The Links between Positive Emotions and Education*, has guided and empowered countless educators in the practice of humor, not only as a personal tool to optimize a healthy lifestyle, but to maximize the benefits of humor in education.

In *Legacy of Laughter: The Playbook,* she adds a new dimension to her earlier work where she identifies five basic stages of humor development. Here she unveils a ground-breaking sixth stage, shedding light on the prenatal origins of humor and the fascinating neuroscience behind it.

*The Playbook* offers an array of playful activities that not only nurture children but also energize adults. She emphasizes and encourages play and playfulness to enhance overall well-being and rejuvenate life, offering a pathway to youthfulness no matter one's age.

Mary Kay's innovation shines throughout, from coining terms such as: *humergy*, which encapsulates the energy that radiates the optimistic joy of our inner spirit, reflects our unique personality, and nourishes a healthy mind/body balance; and *humordoomers*, which describe more serious types.

I am indebted to Mary Kay's immeasurable contribution to the world of humor, and excited that this user-friendly, insightful, and joyful approach will ignite curiosity and spark positive change in the lives of readers worldwide.

In love, laughter, and gratitude,
Ros Ben-Moshe, Author
T*he Laughter Effect: How to Build Joy, Resilience, and Positivity in Your Life*
*Laughing at Cancer: How to Heal with Love, Laughter, and Mindfulness*

# INTRODUCTION

by Mary Kay Morrison

The more I learn about the neuroscience of learning and the benefits of play, the more enthusiastic I am to share what I have learned. Legacy of Laughter: The Playbook explores the significant benefits from a lifetime of engagement in play and playful activities. Shared laughter and joyful play create a lifetime of memories while cultivating positive relationships and nurturing optimal well-being.

My father, William Wiltz, did not actually tell jokes; he playfully enjoyed life. While serving in World War II, he wrote to my mom almost every day. Today those letters and his service are treasured. After the war, he resumed his job as a mail carrier. While he rarely talked about his war experiences, he often exuberantly sang the songs he learned in the military.

> "Play cultivates positive relationships and nurtures optimal well-being."

My mother, Ruth organized our busy and lively household. She creatively led my Girl Scout troupe and arranged piano lessons. The oldest of seven children, I quickly learned to make silly faces as a distraction when diapering a baby or entertaining my siblings on long car trips.

As the first in our family to attend college, I graduated from Northern Illinois University (NIU) with a degree in Early Childhood Education. I embraced my first job as a kindergarten teacher in a high poverty school. I enthusiastically integrated the child development concepts of "learning through play" into the curriculum. However, within a few weeks, administrators advised me that teachers were expected to spend a considerable amount of class time preparing for state and federal tests. Play was not considered to be a part of this experience.

Cognitive research was relatively new at that time, and the school curriculum was based on well-established and traditional instructional programs. This life-changing encounter with a disapproval of *learning through play,* motivated me to dig deeper into brain research. It initiated a life-long journey of exploring the relationship between play and brain development.

During those first years of teaching, I married, had four children, and taught at several different grade levels. We moved when my husband changed careers and joined his family farming business. The next years were filled with a variety of job opportunities including teaching Early Childhood classes at NIU, initiating a hospital clinic for attention deficit (hyperactive) disorder (ADD/ADHD), and working at a community college as a counselor in an adult education program. During this time, I relished participating in a master's program and completing my degree in Adult Education at NIU.

A significant job opportunity was offered to work at an Illinois Regional Office of Education which included providing staff development for more than 200 area schools. This involved the opportunity to attend brain science and mental health conferences and to develop administrative workshops on the neurological benefits of play. My first book, Using Humor to Maximize Learning emerged as a result of the interactions with these educators. In this publication, I created a new term: humergy. Humergy is the energy that emerges from the joy and optimism of our inner spirit, reflects our unique personality, and nourishes a healthy mind/body balance.

> "Humergy is the energy that emerges from the joy and optimism of our inner spirit..."

A conference offering a session on humor in education initiated my participation in the Association for Applied and Therapeutic Humor (AATH). I was honored to be elected president and with support of the board engaged in writing and implementing the initial curriculum for the AATH Humor Academy program. This three-year international HA program served more than 200 learners in the first 15 years.

The research I have conducted on the benefits of play and laughter was reinforced through treasured experiences as a parent of four amazing children and grandparent of 12 incredible children. This has led to the initiation of the Stages of Humor Development, a concept that was originally detailed in my first publication. After some research and at the recommendation of one of my students Jaypee Olivia from the Philippines, I have included an additional stage: the prenatal (Twinkle, Twinkle) stage.

My wish is that you, the reader, will experience your own unique *Legacy of Laughter* as you jump on the rollercoaster of PLAY. Laugh as you engage in the zips and twists of the life-long game of humor.

Cognitive research concepts that are integrated into THE PLAYBOOK include:

▶ All learning goes through our emotional filter.

▶ Play is critical to optimal brain development.

▶ Children grow best with a focus on their strengths.

▶ Trust is the foundation of positive relationships.

▶ Laughter builds trust and fosters positive communication.

# The Experts Agree: Play Promotes a Healthy Life!

*It's better to play than do nothing.* — Confucious

*Play is our brain's favorite way of learning.* — Diane Ackerman

**Share the Laughter**

**Laugh Out Loud**

**CELEBRATE every Day!**

## Unleash Your Power of Play!

# On Becoming a Humor Being

Play tickles the funny bone while nurturing physical strength, mental agility, and social skills. Since play is a trigger for laughter, it is essential for developing a sense of humor. This *Playbook* explores six stages of humor development as described below:

## Six Stages of Humor Development

1. **Twinkle, Twinkle** (prenatal development)—Emerging research suggests that the emotional health of the mother may contribute to the humor development of the child. This state of well-being during pregnancy may include music, movement, and of course laughter.

2. **Peek-a-Boo** (birth to two years)—There is a universal pattern to the initial stage of humor development after birth beginning with infants learning to laugh. When the playful pattern of peek-a-boo is repeated, the baby learns to anticipate and participate in laughter. The process of evoking laughter with infants is initiated across cultures and is a vital characteristic of human development. The peek-a-boo interaction provides a foundation for many subsequent playful activities including the age-old game of "hide and seek."

3. **Knock Knock** (two years to school age)—Pretending, exaggeration, and creativity emerge in this stage. Make-believe activities and imagination are reflected in silly stories and fantasy drawings. Dramatic play usually imitates adult activities. Taboo words and laughter about body parts are common in early childhood. Jokes about elimination and "private" body parts are often accompanied with giggles.

4. **Riddle-Dee-Dee** (early primary years)—A grasp of irony seems to emerge about six years of age as the developing brain begins to comprehend and appreciate the nuances of humor. This is first observed in the understanding and subsequent creating of jokes and riddles. Sharing riddles reflects significant cognitive growth and an appreciation of how language can create shared laughter.

5. **Pun Fun** (later primary years, grades 4–8)—Children at this stage are moving toward an increased understanding of the subtle differences in language. Word play, verbal quips, and the magic of language become a magnet that can captivate kids. Wit emerges when a child can detect and enjoy the language twist in stories. Puns and gentle satire are appreciated at this age. Kids begin to make up jokes followed by hysterical laughing at their own genius.

6. **Joy Flow** (maturing humor style, high school to adult)—The ultimate goal for maturation of a humor being is for optimal growth and self-discovery. It involves the capacity to view life's challenges with optimistic amusement. Becoming aware of one's own sense of humor provides an opportunity to expand humergy through playful humor practice. This experience of laughter's impact supports mental health as the optimal state of Joy Flow. Play is vital, not only for the growth and development of a child, but it is enormously beneficial for adults as well.

*The first five stages of humor development were originally defined in the author's previous books, *Using Humor to Maximize Learning* (Morrison, 2008) and *Legacy of Laughter: A Grandparent Guide and Playbook* (Morrison, 2021).

## The Benefits of Play

The research on the benefits of play, humor, and laughter on child development are quite clear. Play is a key ingredient in promoting brain growth and it is a powerful trigger for laughter. We know from the research that laughter can reduce stress and maximize learning. My life mission has been to not only promote the benefits of play for children, but to change the prevalent ageism mindset that play is just for kids. Humor and laughter are key ingredients for healthy aging. Play is not only invaluable for kids but benefits everyone. The spice of humor and a playful attitude can improve the ability to laugh during life's challenges.

A joyful frame of mind has a powerful impact on the aging process. My lifelong work in humor studies has revealed that a sense of humor has a significant positive impact on a person's well-being. Play (a physical action) and playfulness (an attitude) help nurture a humor being throughout life, and generate the laughter that cultivates our sense of humor and a positive mindset.

Play tickles the funny bone while nurturing physical strength, mental agility, and social skills. Playful interactions are vital not only for the growth and development of a child, but they are incredibly beneficial for adults as well. Both are essential in creating your own special **humergy** and are the foundation for learning at ALL ages. Purposeful engagement in playful activities will contribute to the Joy-Flow stage of humor growth.

The ability to recognize the variances in language is essential for humor development. The capacity to perceive differences between feelings of joy, surprise, silliness, happiness, and sarcasm are all necessary elements for humor development.

## Play the Game of Humor

On the following pages you can learn more about the Six Stages of Humor by playing **The Game of Humor**! Along the way, you will find ideas and inspiration to unleash the power of play in your life and to become that kidult who delights in a playful positive mindset.

I invite you to join me and share the laughter! When we laugh, others catch it! Laughter and play will support the ability to not only survive in a digital world, but to thrive in it.

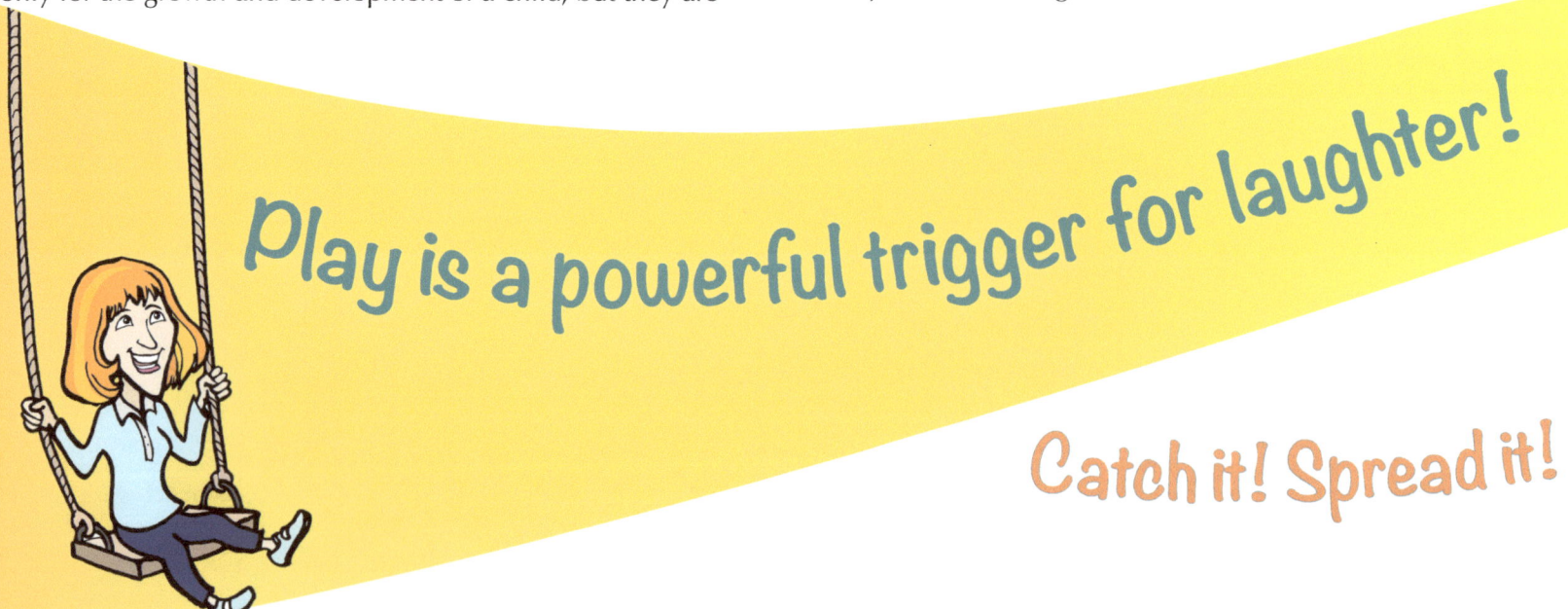

*Play is a powerful trigger for laughter!*

*Catch it! Spread it!*

*Helpful Definitions*

# Humergy

Humergy is extraordinary optimism and a passionate energy for life, combined with a gentle understanding of others. This term describes the energy that radiates the optimistic joy of our inner spirit, reflects our unique personality, and nourishes a healthy mind/body balance (Morrison, 2008).

# Joy Flow

Joy Flow is the degree to which we accomplish optimal growth and self-discovery. This peak experience exemplifies the capacity to view challenges with optimistic amusement. A heightened state of positive emotionality defines this peak experience. Practicing humergy can contribute to a lifelong journey of delight and happiness (Morrison 2008).

# Play and Playfulness

Play and playfulness are critical components for keeping a youthful mindset. Play refers to activities that are spontaneous, enjoyable, and are a vital component of human behavior. Play is observed across all cultures and age groups. Playfulness is an attitude and the ability to find joyful fun in everyday life. Close relationships that include laughter with esteemed family and friends contribute to longevity. These shared joyful experiences provide numerous health benefits.

*Source*: Anthony T. DeBenedet, *Playful Intelligence*.

# Kidult

The term kidult was coined in the 1950s to refer to adults who enjoy children's activities. Join me as a REAL swinger and delight in being a kidult!

# The Game

**How to Play**
Laugh your way through the 6 Stages of Humor until you find your JOY Flow

PLAY tickles your funnybone!

- Sing & Dance
- Rock-a-bye Baby
- Knock Knock
- March to the Music!
- Hunt for birds & bugs
- Highchair water play
- Hang a Colorful Mobile
- Read silly books
- Peek-a-Boo
- Dance to the Music
- Take a Walk
- Sing your favorite tunes
- Massage that baby bump!
- Laugh often
- Twinkle Twinkle

▶ **Start here**
You are a twinkle in your parents' eyes

# ...of Humor

**Engage in Joy Flow**

PRACTICE PRACTICE PRACTICE

Riddle-Dee-Dee • FREE PLAY • Build a Fort • Pun Fun • Hop on a Swing • Plant a Garden • Make Muffins • Draw & Paint • Play Games

Laughter is contagious. It is a RESEARCH-BASED coping skill in the game of life.

## Spin the Wheel

**PLAY triggers Laughter**

Wheel sections: TWINKLE TWINKLE, PEEK A BOO, KNOCK KNOCK, RIDDLE-DEE-DEE, PUN FUN, JOY FLOW

LOL MAGIC

# TWINKLE TWINKLE

## Prenatal Development

Prenatal research indicates that emotional development begins by the 6th month of pregnancy and is affected by the mother's emotions. The womb is not a silent place, and the developing child has the ability to listen, learn, and remember at an ever-evolving level. In utero cognitive development progresses rapidly and is impacted by the experiences of the mother.

The mother can usually feel kicks and movement on a regular basis, and these are often in response to the mother's activities including voices, stories, music and laughter. Research indicates that the baby's heart rate slows in response to the mother's voice. Her voice, laughter, and singing are familiar and after birth these usually have a calming effect.

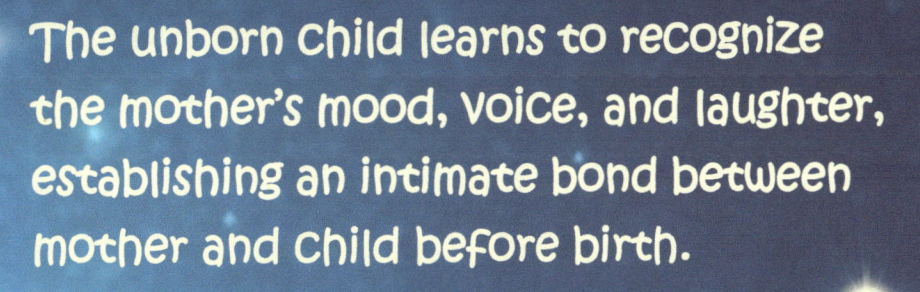

The unborn child learns to recognize the mother's mood, voice, and laughter, establishing an intimate bond between mother and child before birth.

As seen during an ultrasound, if a mom is laughing, the baby bounces around the womb as if on a trampoline.

*There are many origin stories across the globe behind the idea that storks deliver babies. One popular myth emerged in the Netherlands where it was believed that a stork nesting on the roof would bring peace, happiness, and fertility to the household. It became a whimsical and imaginative way to explain to young children the arrival of newborn babies.*

Surround your newborn with love, joy and playful Laughter!

# Peek-a-Boo
## Birth to Two Years

There is a universal pattern to the initial stage of humor development beginning with an infant learning to laugh. The simple game of Peek-a-Boo illustrates the three-part structure. Anxiety followed by surprise leads to relieved laughter.

### 1. Mild Anxiety
Caregiver's face is hidden for a very short time (often with a blanket).

### 2. Surprise
The blanket is taken away to see a smiling caregiver.

### 3. Relief
The child is reassured to see the caregiver and there is shared laughter.

There is a reason that the most popular social media videos feature laughing babies. Laughter is contagious and watching that video provides instant stress relief.

The peek-a-boo interaction with your baby provides a foundation for many subsequent playful activities including the age-old game of Hide and Seek. Surprise will continue to evoke a laughter response throughout life.

The Peek-a-Boo stage builds the foundation of trust and hope that is necessary for emotional intelligence and for building relationships.

1

## Literacy

- Rock and Read, Read, Read: This is absolutely one of the best ways to nurture brain development. *And, it is great for the baby, too!*

- Engage in conversations: Share your favorite childhood memories. Whisper your deep secrets. They will be absorbing language and understand much more than you realize. Bilingual skills are a bonus opportunity for increasing cognitive growth.

- Baby Sign Language: This use of gestures allows infants and toddlers to communicate emotions, desires and needs prior to spoken language. To learn about basic infant sign language, you can find information online.

## Games

- Generate bubbles at bath time by adding a bit of shampoo to the water.

- Manipulate puppets to engage in playful, silly conversations.

- Fill a small plastic bowl with water and put on top of the highchair. Add some mismatched Tupperware pieces, a funnel and/or a plastic strainer. Keep a towel handy.

- Enjoy creative baby toys. The Bumble Ball was our favorite—it generated much adult laughter while it kept Ben and Tyler quite entertained when they started to crawl.

## Music/Drama

- Sing lullabies while rocking to sleep. They will not notice if you are off key!

- Engage in the magic of fingerplays. These short repetitive rhyming phrases include hand movements and will spark your baby's interest. "Where is Thumbkin?" was a favorite.

- Music maximizes brain development. Let them experiment with different instruments.

- Mix the words up in familiar songs. When singing *Old McDonald Had a Farm*, change the "quack, quack" to "meow, meow." This silly adaptation always elicited squeals of laughter from Mimi and shouts of "NOOOO! Ducks go quack!

---

I was singing **You Are My Sunshine** to my 3-year-old and he told me he hates that song. I said that's a shame because I use to sing it to you when you were in my tummy before you were born. He looked me dead in the eyes and said, "I hated it then, too!"

—Anonymous

## Arts and Crafts

▶ Scribbling with crayons can begin at 15 months. Be sure to save a few of these initial works of art with the date.

## Outdoors, Science, and Nature

▶ Observe birds and chat about their songs, color, and species.

▶ Discover butterflies and gently touch caterpillars.

▶ Delight in their first experience of feeling grass and touching flowers.

## Food Stuff

O Put various small pieces of edible foods on their high-chair tray as you are cooking. Talk about the color and texture. Their expressions are priceless photo opportunities.

O Finger painting with pudding seemed like a relatively easy clean-up until I found several chocolate globs in their hair at bath time.

> Use scribble pictures or their artwork to send as thank you notes. Help them write their names on these.
> —Jan Jakeway, friend

# Knock-Knock
## Two Years to School Age

Pretending, exaggeration, and creativity emerge in this stage of humor development. The world of fantasy comes alive. Your kids will become engrossed in make-believe activities with their imagination reflected in silly stories and drawings. Their dramatic play usually imitates adult activities.

Taboo words and laughter about body parts are common in early childhood. Jokes about elimination and "private" body parts are often accompanied with giggles.

At age two-and-a-half Samuel declared that his grandma was sure silly when she sang and exaggerated the movements to several songs. Of course, Samuel was right, as I frequently embellish silly behavior to elicit laughter.

*Imagine... Create*

Kids this age start to engage in conversations.

# Make Music

17

## Literacy

▶ Read silly rhyme books: Dr. Seuss books are a favorite.

▶ Share knock-knock jokes as a way for them to learn comedy patterns.

▶ Expand their vocabulary by reading and playing word games.

▶ Plan field trips to museums, conservatories, and parks.

## Games/Activities

▶ Experiment with a variety of games. Each child has their preferences. While you may want to purchase a few favorites, you can borrow some from your local library to experiment with varied games.

▶ Create a sensory box. Cut hand-sized holes in the top of a shoebox. Put various items inside to touch without being able to see them. Ask if they can guess what is in the box. Try various items: cotton, squishy ball, crayon, spinner, or even an ice cube—anything that would be stimulating to touch.

▶ Create a fort or cave (a large blanket over a small table works well).

▶ Design a playhouse: Cut a door and window into the sides of a huge box. Appliance boxes really are the best. Decorate with crayons or paint.

▶ Create flashlight creatures in a dark room. Start a spooky story and have your child finish the tale.

▶ Suggest a theme: grocery store, doctor office, restaurant. Provide simple props.

## Music/Dance/Drama

▶ Sing silly songs. Add outrageous actions. Old camp songs are usually my first choice.

▶ Rock to the chicken dance or the Hokey Pokey

▶ Attempt Karaoke. Yes—You can!

▶ Play an instrument you learned as a child (dust off that ukulele).

▶ Use songs to encourage picking up toys, washing hands or brushing teeth.

## Arts and Crafts

▸ Make collages by cutting pictures from old magazines. Glue these onto a piece of paper or onto a cut-out brown paper bag. Monitor emerging scissor skills (these small muscle skills develop around the age of 4). Glue sticks are a preferred choice for this age.

▸ Footprint pictures: Paint their feet with acrylic paint, have them step on sturdy paper. Keep a tub of warm water and towels handy. An easier version is to trace around hands for a different creative art experience.

▸ Fashion paper hats, paper airplanes or origami.

## Outdoors, Science, and Nature

▸ Plant a vegetable garden. Put a few small seeds in a container or small dish so they are do not all spill in one garden spot! That combination of water and dirt may be messy but will rapidly accelerate learning.

▸ Simply let them run around outside and scream in delight! Join them.

▸ Arrange for some water play. Fill a large container with water, add some plastic containers, funnels and strainers and let them splash away. Add bubbles for additional wonder.

▸ Take wagon and bike rides. A trip to the neighborhood park can become an unexpected adventure. Ask why is that dog barking and how did that paper end up in the ditch?

▸ Pick flowers. Put individual flowers in between waxed paper and press in a large book. Add some weight on top. When dry, these can be glued in a collage on black paper. Dandelions are always a treasured gift from children. Put them in a vase with water.

▸ Capture caterpillars or insects and create a "hotel" for these little creatures. Let the kids know that the hotel is only good for a short visit. Talk about the importance of a release so they can go back to their own homes. It can be traumatic for young children to find a dead bug in the jar.

*Ben and Tyler really enjoy blowing bubbles outside.*

*Music maximizes brain development. Let them experiment with different instruments.*

## Cooking with Children

▶ Make a pot of Stone Soup. Start with a stone* and proceed using the various ingredients mentioned in the book. Add vegetable broth or bouillon cubes.

*Note: Bleach a smooth stone and boil it in a separate pot before using it in the soup.*

▶ Carve a pumpkin, scoop out the seeds and toast. Toss with a bit of butter and salt. Bake for 40 minutes at 300 degrees.

▶ Discover the star in an apple. Cut an apple horizontally to see the "star." There are several wonderful children's books that can supplement this activity. Dip the slices in peanut butter for a nutritious snack.

▶ Peel a potato or carrot. Start by demonstrating how to push the peeler away from the body.

▶ Follow a recipe that they have chosen. Encourage them to read some of the words. Making tapioca with Cloe involved discussing the difference between tablespoons and teaspoons.

▶ Wash dishes. Pull a stool up to the sink so they can enjoy washing the plastic dishes over and over again. "This is my favorite thing to do" Faith, age 6.

▶ Create edible plate art. Arrange food in different shapes to create animals, flowers or other objects. Pinterest has more ideas than you can try in a lifetime.

*Stone Soup*

# EGGS!

*Cooking – A super skill to learn!*

## Learning to CRACK an egg.

Teach them to crack an egg (as early as 16 months). They will take huge delight in seeing what is inside the egg. Keep a wet cloth available to wipe their hands.

Steve was always happy when he was successfully able to crack the egg into a bowl without any shells. "My kids loved baking with you: breaking eggs was a BIG DEAL when they were little."

Julie, daughter-in-law- Steve's mom

## Smoochie Moochie

Isha is a puppet who lives in cherry juice.

He puts his ears onto his eyes when he is in the juice.

He can see with his ears.

He has an eyeball in his mouth.

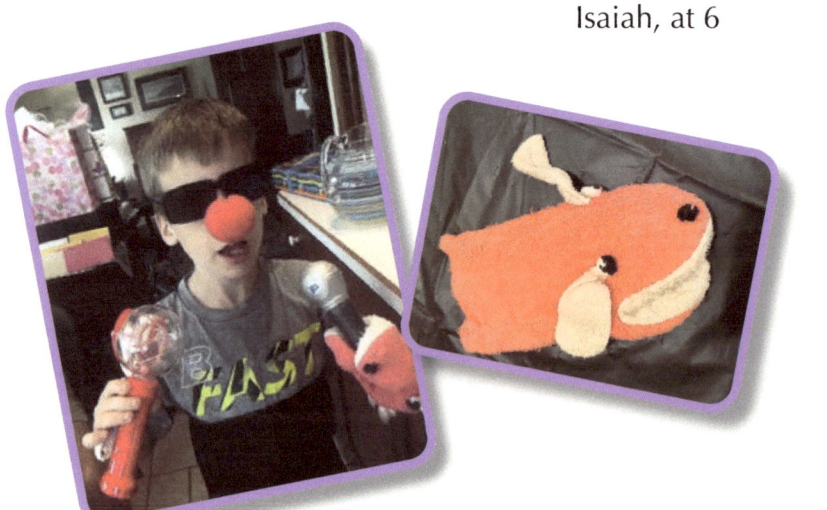

*Isaiah, at 6*

Create a story using puppets. Sock puppets can be easily created from that collection of mismatched socks. This is one of my favorite stories that was created when Isaiah discovered an old well-worn pink puppet at our house.

# Riddle-Dee-Dee
## Early Primary Years

You are a superhero to your child. Use your super powers to persuade some device downtime. A powerful persuasion activity is reading together, sharing stories, and repeating those activities that you enjoy together.

Food preparation is usually a huge hit. Tempt your child with nature exploration, art and music, and vigorous physical activity.

Parents and other close family members can have a significant role in modeling humor and interjecting laughter into difficult situations. There are many strategies you can use to initiate fun into conversations with your children.

Practice riddles, laugh at their silly antics, and read funny books. A grasp of irony seems to emerge about six years of age and riddles and jokes will be appreciated.

What did the ocean say to the beach??
NOTHING! It just waved.

# Laugh Outloud

## 3

"What did the little corn say to the mama corn?"

Where is POP corn?

"What is a tree's favorite drink?"

Root beer!

## Jokes, Riddles, Comic Books, Stories, Puppets, Snacks

### Literacy

- Introduce joke and riddles! Even reluctant readers will be tempted to try reading joke, riddle and comic books. Let them practice the joke and riddles on you.
- Post some riddles on the refrigerator door. Invite them to figure out the answer. Before they come, put a variety of riddles on index cards and see if they can solve them. Let them take these home to try on their parents.
- Find creative ways to help with homework: Learn spelling words by drawing the letters on the ceiling with a flashlight.
- Attend funny movies. There are many great children's movies that have subtle underlying humor specifically intended for the adults watching the film. Afterwards ask them about the funniest part of the movie. Invite them to write a movie review.

### Games/Activities

- Board and card games are a MUST at this age. Our favorites include: Apples to Apples, Blank Slate, and Tapple.
- Plan ahead for activities when traveling in the car. Wrap presents for each child to open when boredom sets in. Create travel BINGO sheets or do the alphabet game where starting with finding something that starts with the letter "A" and continuing through "Z." Can also look for the actual letter if it is impossible to find the letter "X" for example.
- We always have snacks during family games—popcorn is a favorite.
- Day Trip Adventures: Plan ahead!
- Library: Not only a great place to find books, but an invaluable resource for programs and activities.
- County Fairs: Review the schedule of events and consider attendance during the kid's day programs.
- Museum events: Search for special events and upcoming exhibits. Family passes are often available.
- A zoo trip is always captivating. Check out the feeding schedules online before you go.

*Say yes to amusement park rides—unless they want to do the death defying roller coaster!*

# Learning emerges from the process.

## Music/Drama

▶ Form a Marching Band: Play lively parade music. Supply a variety of home-made instruments and encourage them to march. This is a great activity for cousins.

▶ Get sing-along books for the car.

▶ Find a family theme song (for our 12 grands—it was the 12 days of Christmas). Enact the song or create dance routines.

▶ Dance parties: Just put on some dance music and exhibit your best moves. They will join in or roll their eyes and laugh! Share the dance moves you learned in high school and they will laugh again.

▶ Invite your child to play their instrument. Andrew often entertained us with his guitar and Emma with her flute.

## Arts and Crafts

▶ Finger paint by spraying shaving cream on a baking sheet. This activity is an easy clean-up! Use old t-shirts to protect clothes.

▶ Design a fairy garden. Visit a greenhouse for ideas and supplies. Our local venue donated some clean dirt for the base and pebbles for the paths. A large boot or shoebox works well for a first attempt. Fill with sand or dirt and watch their imaginations flourish. Faith loved creating her special garden and rearranges the fairy figures over and over again.

▶ Play-Doh®: I usually buy this at the dollar store but there are recipes online to create your own. Provide a variety of measuring cups and small plates. Use a marker to create "burners" on top of an empty shoe box so they can "cook" you a meal. Emma always enjoyed making food for us to taste. Of course, we took great delight in letting her know that it was delicious . . . or that it needed more salt.

Faith's Fairy Garden

## Outdoors, Science and Nature

▶ Go on a toad hunt. Use a net and bring a container. Look for these elusive creatures under rocks and in swampy areas.

▶ Katie caught a toad for Cloe at our house. Toadie now lives in an amphibian house in her bedroom. There have been several toads caught in our yard and so I just saved the container for any captured creatures.

▶ Climb
- Climbing trees are so much fun.
- Rock climbing is also a great adventure.
- Faith testing her balance when she climbed up on the stone wall.

▶ Capture lightening bugs (fireflies). Demetra and Jaime, our nieces from California, had never experienced these delightful creatures and were enchanted to see them light up in a glass jar.

▶ Look for and identify birds. See if you can find a nest or a feather. Try to guess what kind of bird it belonged to. Bird books help to identify the birds at the feeder.

▶ Science experiments can be fun. Experiment with making volcanoes, shoot rockets, or explore what happens with air currents from ceiling fans.

We use the fire pit often. Mary Kay gathers the supplies for S'mores, and I get the fire ready for roasting marshmallows. The cold fire pit also was a haven for toads and the kids like to dig through the coals to find them.

Don Morrison

## Cooking with Children

▶ Read the book *Stone Soup* (again). I know I am repeating this activity—it has been one of the most requested activities from our grandchildren.

▶ Try blindfold taste tests. Buy several varieties of apples and discuss which is the tartest or sweetest. See if they can guess the flavor of green grape versus the purple grape. Taste test different flavors of yogurt.

▶ Create Monster Pancakes. This was the number one favorite breakfast every morning of overnight stays at our house.

Another thing we did was monster pancakes. Now these were of course, pancakes, with a twist. Chocolate chips, craisins and nuts arranged into a face with syrup and on top. Delicious, messy and fun. These were perfect and a great part of my childhood.

Favorite memory from Ben

### Isaiah's Muffin Maker Story

I woke up at 5:25 a.m. I went downstairs, and Grandma warmed up the oven while we sat and talked with the lions. (Grandma note—yep, these are stuffed animals). I put the cupcake liners in the pan. And I helped Grandma put the dough in the liners. I put the drizzle of brown sugar and butter on the muffins. Then Grandma put the muffins in the oven. Grandpa came in the kitchen and he said, "Yum, yum, yum."

Isaiah, at 6

# Pun Fun
## Later Primary Years, Grades 4-8

Long fairy tales have a tendency to dragon.

Children at this stage are moving toward an increased understanding of the subtle differences in language. Word play, poetic adaptions, and the magic of the English language become a magnet that can captivate children from age 10 through teen years.

Observe when your child can first detect and enjoy a language twist in stories. Notice when they are able to "get the joke." Puns and gentle satire are appreciated at this age. They may begin to make up their own jokes and they will laugh hysterically at their own genius.

Do not be afraid to try crazy, out-of-the box activities. Keeping plans a secret until the day of the activity adds to the suspense and fun. Kids love to guess what you have planned for surprises on their special day.

The middle years initiate the emergence of puberty, with jokes about sex and the emergence of hormonal behavior. Adolescents experience anxiety about the physical changes they experience, and sexual humor can provide relief from the stress of puberty. Physical growth evokes a challenges for preteens, who resort to laughing with others as a coping device. Unfortunately, it is often a stage where peers might laugh at them, not with them. Many teens experience or participate in bullying behavior.

Playful teasing can be fun when there is mutual trust. Discuss the difference between playful teasing and bullying. "If the impact is hurtful, it is inappropriate, even if the intent is not harmful" (Morrison, 2008). At this age they start to create jokes to let you know that they are kidding.

Gift them with books written specifically for teens. My favorite is: "Find Your Funny: The Humor Survival Guide" by Barb Best & Joanne Jackal.

The best April Fool jokes are the ones that keep on giving. One year, I went to my daughter's house when the family was gone and attached googly eyes to everything in the cupboard and refrigerator. When they pulled out the milk carton or cereal box, they found silly eyes staring at them. Googly eyes can be put on virtually anything—toothpaste tubes, lampshades, and laundry detergent, even a love note slipped into a pocket!

Kathy Laurenhue, friend, from Wiser Now newsletter

I am usually not surprised when Grandma does something unusual or out of the box, something most Grandmas don't do.

Christine, age 11

*Explore the element of surprise.*

## Literacy

- Joke books are a must! Cartoons and memes are fun to send via text.
- Create vision boards to assist with memory work. Using old magazines, cut out pictures related to the subject to be learned. Glue the pictures onto a poster board or into a study assistance notebook. Invite them to create a riddle or joke about the lesson.

## Games

- In-house Hide and Seek—a favorite is "Sardines" where one person hides, and everyone tries to find them. When found, they hide with them until the last person finds the group. This has been a favorite game for Samuel. They like to hide in closets; be prepared to find clothes that fell off their hangers on the floor. One year, Steve hid under the Christmas tree.
- Charades are fun with children, especially when they create the challenge words.
- Lego kits or puzzles are quieter activities that can be fun one-on-one.
- Board games are great fun for the entire family. Some of our favorites: Blurt, Monopoly, Yahtzee, Pictionary, Mega Mouth.

## Music/Drama

- Host a cousin movie night at your house. Have a popcorn bar with nuts and various toppings.
- Several of the pre-teens have asked to play their favorite radio station when we are driving. Commercials are a great time to discuss the lyrics and learn more about current teen music and culture.
- Invite children to write a basic screenplay and enact it.
- Concerts, plays, and movies are great options. Emma was excited for a trip to the Fireside Theater for a dinner theater event with her mom and grandparents.

*The games Blurt, Mega Mouth (pictured above), and Tribond were created by my friend Tim Walsh, co-founder of Roo Games.*

*The best part about jazz band is when you have anxiety that your solo won't go well but then it sounds amazing.*

— Steve, at 13

## Arts and Crafts

▶ Enroll in an art class together. Christine and I enjoyed taking an oil class together at Nicholas Conservatory.

▶ Paint with acrylics on a variety of materials. This is a good age to experiment with painting on canvas or wood. Steve painted an amazing rooster for me to add to the large collection of roosters in my house. Rock monsters can be painted, sprayed with lacquer, and placed in an outdoor garden.

▶ Try block-print art using cut potatoes, leaves, or even fish.

▶ Experiment with different art materials. A package of pipe cleaners can offer endless opportunities. Oil pastels and clay are great mediums to introduce at this age.

## Outdoors, Science, and Nature

▶ Stargazing: There are intriguing apps that can help identify the night sky. Lie on a blanket on the ground and use a flashlight to point out the stars. Be sure to share the story of the milky-way and other constellations.

▶ Forest preserves and conservation districts offer endless opportunities for nature walks, exhibits and programs.

▶ Spontaneous play is such fun. It is especially exciting when there is an announcement that school is closed for the day. A snow day can provide unanticipated fun time spent in the outdoors!

## Foodstuff

▶ Request that they make a dish for the family gathering. Christine made a delicious Baked Alaska for one of our Christmas parties. It was fun for all of us to watch her start it on fire.

▶ Invite your grandchild to make and submit recipes for a family cookbook that includes their favorite food ideas. When we made homemade macaroni and cheese together, Tyler added a secret ingredient to this recipe. It is a now a family favorite.

▶ Host a fancy meal. Plan the menu and prep the food together. Set the table, create a centerpiece, and take out the fancy dishes. Invite the grandkids to help clean up after the meal. Play lively music, sing or dance while doing the dishes.

▶ At a family gathering ask for assistance with taking dessert orders from the adults. Children are delighted when they can add add sky-high mounds of ice cream or whipped cream.

*Cloe spent hours creating collages including this girl on a swing which hangs from the ceiling in her room.*

Day 5 — Maximizes Joyful Living

# Joy Flow

## Maturing Humor Style— High School to Adult

The ultimate goal for maturation of a humor being is for optimal growth and self-discovery. A humor being views life's challenges with optimistic amusement. A heightened state of positive emotionality is the goal of this stage.

When adults are having fun and laughing, they provide a positive model for children. Playing with kids will add life to your years. Becoming aware of one's own sense of humor provides an opportunity to expand humergy through humor practice. This experience of laughter's flow and the emerging energy will create a natural euphoric high that will be a model for your grandchild.

If a family continues to engage in playful interactions and shared laughter, all will benefit. Let your family and friends know that you appreciate the laughter they bring to your life.

## Literacy

▶ Encourage your grandchildren to write about their memories with you. Create a book with these memories. Notice what happened to me with this process! You might just write a book like I did!

▶ Read funny obituaries together. Notice how frequently humor is mentioned as an admired attribute when memorializing a life. Humor and laughter are indeed a legacy that is frequently shared at memorials. Read an obituary about someone you knew, share it with your grandchild along with your favorite memories. This is an opportune time to initiate a conversation about grief. You may be one of the few people who will have this kind of opportunity to discuss this difficult topic. Remind them that laughter is what people often remember about the loved one who has died.

*Emotional intelligence is a factor in appreciating and learning to use humor.*

## Games

▶ Along with previous suggestions- here are some others that our teenagers enjoy.

▶ Scavenger Hunt: Emma designed her own version of a scavenger hunt when we were on our 8th grade trip and had to wait in the small airport. She walked around with her grandpa, finding unique items or signs. She made a creative list of things for me to find. It was a great activity to keep us entertained in what could have been a long wait time in a boring airport.

▶ Board and Cards are a great way to connect with teens. Favorites include: Pit, Scrabble, Telestrations, 5 Crowns, Spoons, and 7-Up (card game).

## Music/Dance/Drama

▶ Dance together with a music video that illustrates the moves.

▶ Attend a live dinner theater production.

> When I went to Grandma's house, we had a tradition of playing card games, the most popular is 7-Up. While I wasn't terrible at it, I had fallen into a trend where I would lose no matter what. After about three years, I finally broke that losing streak. NO matter what I always ended up having fun.
>
> **Tyler, at 17**

### Arts and Crafts

▶ Make hand crafted greeting cards.

▶ Do silhouette self-portraits. Tape paper to the wall. Use a flashlight to outline the face on black paper. Cut and paste on white background.

▶ Plan a trip to an art museum and request any education materials to optimize the learning. The Chicago Art Museum has educational materials and programs for students. Samuel really enjoyed finding works of art on the recommended list.

### Outdoors, Science, and Nature

▶ Sprinklers and water projectiles: teenagers especially enjoy dousing each other with an unexpected water spraying.

▶ Water balloon toss contests can be quite animated. Be prepared to get wet.

▶ Initiate flashlight adventures at night. Hide and Seek and/or scavenger hunts in the dark can be thrilling. An open field is the perfect place for flashlight tag.

▶ Fire pit activities include camp songs, cooking kabobs, or roasting marshmallows for s'mores.

▶ Tree climbing, hiking, and ziplining can be an awesome challenge, especially for the grandparent. Emma requested that we go zip-lining for her 8th grade trip. It was scary for all of us, but a ton of fun.

▶ Indoor rock climbing walls and trampoline parks are perfect for tweens and teens, especially in bad weather.

▶ Rent paddle boats or canoes. Insist that they wear safety vests.

▶ Fly kites. Blow bubbles. Toss bean bags. Throw balls.

▶ Catch worms at night for fishing the next day. Turn the hose on for an hour and the worms will come close to the surface.

▶ National Parks are amazing places to hike. We saw a black bear near the trail on Emma's 8th grade trip.

### Foodstuff

▶ Plan a "Create Your Own ___" party. Provide basic ingredients and a variety of toppings for everyone to make their own. Some ideas: Pizza, Taco, Baked Potato, Ice Cream, Popcorn and Candy.

▶ Grill cheese sandwiches and serve with tomato soup.

▶ Monster pancakes never get old!

# Embrace Your Extraordinary Sauce

Each person will devise their own special recipe for bringing the gift of laughter into the lives of others. Embrace that unique sauce! Treasure each opportunity for nurturing your treasured relationships and making a significant impact in their lives.

In order to provide optimal care for yourself and others it is essential to take care of YOU! Balancing expectations and new challenges can be both exhilarating and exhausting. Your health is a vital aspect for spending quality time with family and friends. Carefully consider your energy, interests, and capabilities.

*Maximize the joyful magic of this new journey with self-care:*

- ▶ **Maximize Fitness:** If you are not working out, today is a good time to start! You will be able to do more activities and sustain your well-being if you are fit. Simple weightlifting, and a cardio routine are highly recommended. If you are not already working out, get going! You are not too old, and it is never too late.

- ▶ **Maximize Time:** Look at your current schedule for any adjustments that you might want to make to include for travel with children for both short adventures and longer trips. I find it helpful to have numerous "surprises" ready for unexpected playmates and guests. It is helpful to offer kids a list of choices for activities. One idea is to write some ideas on slips of paper and have them draw these (one at a time) out of your "Surprise Jar."

> "I really don't mind getting older, but my body is taking it badly."

*Suggestions to fill your Surprise Jar:*
- Choose an art project ( have some supplies on hand-crayon. paste and colored construction paper)
- Play age-appropriate games (again give choices)
- Take a nature walk
- Read their favorite book
- Sing songs or dance to music
- Feed birds-catch bugs
- Prepare lunch: Have recipes and ingredients ready

- ▶ **Maximize Healthy Eating:** Enjoy more blueberries, salmon, and chocolate (especially chocolate.) Not only good for you, but a powerful example for children. Not sure how well I am doing with modeling this. My teenage grandkids think that trail mix is M&M's with obstacles.

- ▶ **Maximize Positivity:** Begin a journal and record your playful journey. Look for the humor in everyday life and the ability to see funny! As you get older, you've got to stay positive. For instance, the other day, I fell down the stairs. Instead of getting upset, I thought, "Wow, That's the fastest I've moved in years."

## How to Create Your Hot Sauce

Hot means full of spicy energy and enthusiasm. Make your sauce as hot as possible by living life to the fullest. The definition of play (frolic) is to "jump for joy" or to "move about energetically!"

You are uniquely equipped to enrich your life and that of others with your own creative version of energized play. Play is integral to learning new skills at all ages. Incorporating playfulness into your relationships is a purposeful, stimulating, and splendid responsibility. It also brings great satisfaction. Don't be afraid of being silly or looking ridiculous. Have courage! This is the perfect opportunity for you to try new adventures. Romp like you have springs in your legs—even if they are bionic. Somehow children bring out the desire to frolic, even if it means you will challenge them to a race from your wheelchair. Of course, they need a "handicap" and will need to hop backwards or even walk on their hands!

> **PLAY is the foundation for learning for ALL ages. Enhancing your own playful spirit by nurturing your hot sauce will be your unique legacy of laughter for the children in your life.**
> —Mary Kay Morrison

How do you find the laughter in your life? In my book *Using Humor to Maximize Learning*, I defined the experience of vigorous, optimistic energy as **humergy**. Facing the tough stuff with a sense of humor is a powerful strategy for coping with life challenges. Laughter reduces stress and depression. An ability to find the funny in life will help provide your very own spicy ingredients to serve up for the children in your life. Of course, they will inspire you, too!

### Ideas to incorporate laughter into your life:

- Watch funny movies. Share your favorites.
- Read humorous books/magazines (include joke/riddle books).
- Share memes and funny posts on social media.
- Create a journal, story, or poem about the hilarious stuff. Kids can be endless source of mirth.
- Find friends who make you laugh, and plan activities with them. Recreate a childlike birthday party for you or your friends. Be sure to include kites, bubbles, and yo-yos.
- Bring playfulness into everyday life. Remember what you did as a child that brought joy and laughter. Try that activity again. I am a REAL swinger, and we have five swings in our yard that invigorate my playful childhood spirit.
- Expand your knowledge by taking classes and expand your knowledge base on topics you would like to explore.
- Find organizations that purposefully incorporate play and laughter during challenging times. My favorite is *The Association for Applied and Therapeutic Humor*, a nonprofit international organization whose mission is to study, practice, and promote healthy humor. Sign up for their complimentary newsletter.
- Make snow angels!

*Embrace Each Day!*

## How will you be remembered?

The loving support that comes from close relationships is vital for optimal wellness. You can have a significant role in nurturing a humor being. Purposeful engagement in playful activities will generate lifelong memories. Play tickles the funny bone while nurturing physical strength, mental agility, and social skills. These interactions are vital not only for the growth and development of a child, but are incredibly beneficial for adults as well. You can provide your own unique hot sauce creating an enduring *Legacy of Laughter* for generations to come.

# References

## Publications

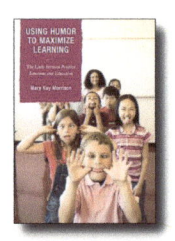

Morrison, M.K. (2008). Using Humor to Maximize Learning: The Links between Positive Emotions and Education, Rowman & Littlefield Education, USA.

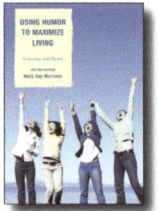

Morrison, M.K. (2012). Using Humor to Maximize Living: Connecting with Humor, R&L Education, USA.

Morrison, M.K. (2021). Legacy of Laughter: A Grandparent Guide and Playbook, Humor Quest, USA.

### Most recent research

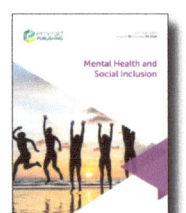

Humor, Laughter and Mental Health; A Case Study of Mary Kay Morrison is an autoethnography published by the *Journal of Mental Health and Social Inclusion* with co-authors Mary Kay Morrison, Ros Ben-Moshe, and Freda Gonot-Schoupinsky.

**Findings:** Mary Kay recommends exploration of the benefits of humor and laughter for mental health professionals. She coined the terms *Humergy* (a joyful, optimistic, healthy energy) and *Humordoomer* (a person who zaps that energy from us).

## About the Author

The quest to increase her knowledge of parenting, education, and learning led to the pursuit of a master's degree in Adult Education. Mary Kay was captivated with the concept of lifelong learning and in these classes realized that her experiences as a parent and educator provided a unique perspective on the importance of humor and play. With a large and growing family, she experienced first-hand the critical importance of practicing playfulness as a survival skill in the everyday struggle of balancing work, classes, and family life.

A former kindergarten teacher with a passion for understanding the neuroscience of learning, Mary Kay has been writing and speaking for more than 40 years about the critical importance of play for optimal growth and development.

As a college professor who designed and teaches a course in humor studies that promotes the health benefits of humor, Mary Kay realizes that playful activities not only support learning but nurture the development of a sense of humor.

The grandmother of 12 beautiful, amazing, incredible grandchildren (she's not shy about bragging), Mary Kay has found countless ways to interact and play with them over the past 24 years. Their written contributions and those of their parents are an integral part of this book.

The first *Legacy of Laughter: A Grandparent Guide and Playbook* was written to share her knowledge and encourage grandparents to explore the benefits of play with their grandchildren.

She received numerous requests for a follow up Playbook designed not just for grandparents, but for everyone who interacts with kids. Thus, *Legacy of Laughter: The Playbook* was born.

# FUNdamental Ideas, Resources, and Supplies

This is a quick go-to list of ideas, supplies and resources to support play-filled learning. While many of these are noted throughout the book under the various stages of humor development, we've put together this comprehensive list since many of the activities cross developmental stages. You can use this as a checklist when shopping or when asked for gift ideas. Numerous low-cost options are included. Many of our most popular items have been GARAGE SALE FINDS! A gazillion resources and other ideas can be found online.

## The Basics

- Sturdy kid table and chairs (or picnic table): Basic resource for countless activities.
- Special drawer: Kids often like to be in the area where you are working—designate a special drawer for them stocked with art supplies, magnets, magnifying glasses, prisms, slinkies, art supplies, flashlights, and puzzle books, etc. **HINT:** Put in a few at a time; rotate often.
- Surprise jar: Recycle a large plastic container and label SURPRISE JAR. Fill with suggestions for activities. I use index cards to write these ideas on. Numerous ideas are listed below. Include their favorite ideas suggestions. When they say they are bored, invite them to draw a card. **RULE:** If they choose to draw, they must follow through with the suggested activity. Or they can draw 2 cards—but must do one.
- Magazine subscriptions: For fun new reading material, a subscription to a children's magazine is a wonderful suggestion to relatives/friends for a holiday or birthday gift.

## Imagination Stations

- Grocery Store
  - Cash register, play money, grocery cart
  - Shelves stocked with empty food boxes, egg cartons, clean milk containers, and plastic spice containers.
  - Recycled grocery bags: kids enjoy being the "cashier."
- Dress-up trunk or box (*What's in your closet?*)
  - Hats, briefcases, shoes
  - Purses with notebooks, keyrings, wallets
  - Brightly colored clothing, scarves
  - Halloween costumes, wigs
  - Old phones, electronic devices
  - Small suitcase or gym bag
- Hotel
  - Plastic hotel keys can serve as "credit cards."
- Hospital
  - Medical supplies (band-aids, surgical masks, rubber gloves, old bottles, etc.). Use an old blanket to cover a bed.
- Restaurant
  - Dishes, plastic silverware, napkins
  - Menus
  - Play food
- Forts or Playhouses
  - Big empty boxes: Recycle refrigerator or stove boxes for playhouses. **HINT:** Adult help needed in cutting out the doors and windows.
  - Large sheets or blankets over a table can create a tent or house.

## *Large and Small Muscle Activities*

- Manipulatives
  - Legos (classic sets encourage creativity)
  - Recycle plastic containers
  - Dominos effect (create a cascading ripple movement)
- Games, playing cards, and puzzles
- Large muscle toys: large blocks, trucks, scooters, wagons

## *Arts and Crafts*

- Individual tote: Fill with pencils, crayons, construction paper, glue, and scissors. They can create their own "office."
- Paints: Acrylics are perfect for kids (be sure they are no longer putting their fingers in their mouths). **HINTS:** 1) A cheap plastic tablecloth on the table and/or on the floor is recommended; 2) Paper plates work well with plastic knives for mixing paints; and 3) Make a game out of cleaning the brushes. See if they can clean so well that NO color comes on a blank paper after cleaning the brushes.
- Paint rocks and add uplifting words. Place in outdoor parks and playgrounds so others have the joy of finding them.
- Playdoh: Find these at $Dollar stores or check out recipes online for making your own. **HINT:** To minimize mess, spread a large tarp or recycled sturdy plastic tablecloth. Also works well in an outdoor area (porch or deck).
- Spray shaving cream onto a cookie sheet for quick clean-up finger painting.
- Multicolored pipe cleaners are fun and a great car activity.
- Sidewalk chalk: Create welcome signs for company or invite neighborhood kids to join the creative chalk project.
- Stickers: Create a sticker book with recycled paper, or use a small spiral-bound notebook.
- Recycled mail, holiday cards, and magazines are perfect for cut and paste activities.

## *Music and Dance*

- Instruments:
  - Home-made shakers: Put rice, dried lentils (or other dried beans) inside empty toilet paper rolls and firmly tape the ends with wide masking tape. Different fillers make different sounds.
  - Drums created from empty oatmeal containers are fun.
  - Kazoo: cheap from the $Dollar store. A good outdoor activity.
  - Harmonica: birthday sections often offer these in 6-packs along with other fun stuff like slinkies and bubbles.
  - Rain sticks: create from paper towel rolls or clean empty soda bottles. Fill with different sized pebbles and duct tape ends.

## *Outdoor Items*

- Child-size picnic table
- Large plastic tub for water play (add old Tupperware, bottles, and funnels)
- Wagon (a garden cart can double as a kid wagon)
- Bikes (if you get inexpensive bikes at garage sales, remember to check the tires as they are expensive to replace)
- Garden tools and child size gloves
- Bug catchers and butterfly nets
- Swings: Tire swings in trees are a huge hit; teenagers enjoy pushing each other and twisting the circle swings til dizzy.
- Kites, bubbles, bean bags, balls
- Balloons for balloon toss (the kind you can fill 10 at a time)
- Corn hole, bean bag toss
- Pogo sticks, hula hoops

# Acknowledgments

To my sweet husband Don, whose love and encouragement are the foundation for my inspiration and endeavors.

Never-ending gratitude for my amazing children, William (Jennifer), Andy (Julie), Rachael (Jason) and Peter (Val); for these incredible grandchildren, Ben, Tyler, Andrew, Samuel, Emma, Mimi, Christine, Katie, Stephen, Cloe, Isaiah, and Faith; and for my extended family.

Beyond grateful for the creative genius of my LOL editor, Deborah McKew, who realized the vision for my books before I did. For Kyle Edgell, the LOL graphic designer who is one of the most extraordinary artists that I am privileged to call my friend and colleague.

Blessed with my dear friend, Ros Ben Moshe, who initiated the publication of my ethnography research publication and has written the significant foreword and testimonial to this book.

Ecstatic and beyond grateful for the remarkable endorsements from Anthony DeBenedet, Tim Walsh, Mary Cousin, and Karyn Buxman. So thankful for the amazing testimonials from those who share my passion for play: Brenda Elsagher, Anne Pratt, Freda Gonot-Schoupinksy, Pat Rumbaugh, and Joyce Saltman.

Grateful also to Freda Gonot-Schoupinksy for inspiring my ethnography research article highlighting my work in the book: *The Positive Psychology of Laugher and Humour*.

My experience in humor research would not have been possible without my AATH friends and colleagues: Roberta Gold, Barbara Grapstein, Cathy Grippi, David Jacobson, Jennifer Keith, Allen Klein, Miyuki Kobayashi, Masako Kusakari, Mary Laskin, Kathy Laurenhue, Kathy Luhn, Tabatha Mauldin, Melissa Mork, Nila Nielsen, Katherine Puckett, J, Michele St. Clair, Steve Sultanoff, Kathy Velasco, Heather Walker, Stacy Wallace, Laurie Young.

Recognition goes to the more than 300 HA students in the Humor Academy especially Jaypee Olivia who insisted that I needed the prenatal stage of Humor Development, even suggesting the title of the first stage as "Twinkle, Twinkle."

Kudos to my local author friends in the *Last Tuesday Author Club* including Karla Clark, Sandy Colbert, Catherine Conroy, Kelly Epperson, Marie Maliki, Melissa McCormick, and Kristin Oakley.

Grateful for YMCA colleagues, Mary Urbelis, and my PiYo exercise support class.

Kudos to Michael Harris, videographer for his belief in my work and for the book promo interview, and to Annie P. Ruggles for the support in social media coaching.

## For more information, swing by Humor Quest:

www.questforhumor.com

where you will find lots of additional information and resources

**Mary Kay Morrison**
*Educator, Author, Speaker*

*Founder and Director, AATH Humor Academy*

Printed in the USA
CPSIA information can be obtained
at www.ICGtesting.com
JSHW040148180724
66551JS00002B/2